SPEAKIN
THE DE

Speaking of the Dead

M.R. PEACOCKE

Happy writing,
Richie.

Meg

PETERLOO POETS

First published in 2003
by Peterloo Poets
The Old Chapel, Sand Lane, Calstock, Cornwall PL18 9QX, U.K.

© 2003 by M.R. Peacocke

**A catalogue record for this book is available
from the British Library**

ISBN   1-904324-06-1

Reprinted 2004, 2005
Printed and bound by Antony Rowe Ltd, Eastbourne

ACKNOWLEDGEMENTS

Acknowledgements are due to the editors of the following journals in which some of these poems first appeared: *Critical Quarterly, The London Magazine, The North, The Oxford Magazine, Pitch, Poetry Review, The Rialto, Tabla.*

Remembering three friends:
Elizabeth, Dorothy, Phyl.

Contents

A Glass of Water

I wanted to show you a glass
filled with a measure of water.
No history in this glass no irony
but the dailiness of the tap
in a moulded vessel, daylight
coming in blue coming in green
through water and thickness of glass.
But how to show you not my face
in the quaking disc nor thirsty longings
nor mystery nor parable nor glaze
of recollection, not to perceive it
even as a lens but as a plain glass
of water? How to be naked enough
to attend to a thing in its presence?

John Clare Watches a Snail

I observed a snail on his journey at full speed
and I marked by my watch that he went 13 inches
in 3 minutes, which was the utmost he could do
without stopping to wind or rest.

Here's an old woman planting out potatoes.
One is safely set. She's straightening her back
before she chooses the next well-chitted spud
and shuffles along two boots' worth
and hoops herself over and dibbles and plants
and treads round a little and repeats it all
without stopping to wind or rest.
Her shadow has travelled round her,
contracting and expanding. Sphere within sphere,
everything's on the move. To gauge the music
you must be still for a long time and uncurl
helical distance by the light of a watch.

John Clare one Springtime

April 2001

When John Clare passed my gate that April day
I saw he was weeping. Would you like a cup of tea?
but Oh the poor children he cried, rubbing his face
on a dusty sleeve. What children? The ones
that've dropped their coats in the field, how cold they'll be,
their woollen jackets bleaching in the wind and rain,
and their mothers will scold them. No, John, I said,
don't grieve for the children. They'll be warm.
It's the lambs you saw by the wall, the slaughtered lambs.

Firing Day

Far off, the guns sound
like laundry flapping. Listen
to the peaceful guns.

Up on the high fell
nothing waves or warns except
a red flag or two.

There are peregrine,
dunlin it's said and black grouse
where nobody walks.

Sheep don't disturb them.
Live ammo in the heather
makes no stumbling block.

We value greatly,
the Colonel writes, our record
of conservation.

(He carries very
powerful binoculars
like a gamekeeper.

He counts the number
of angels perched on the pin
of a ripe grenade.)

Lunch Break

The point in the little park, shaven
brown a green blade or two yellow grass
random with metallic and paper scraps
and bleached turds of errant dogs,
at which she abandons choosing and sits down
and opens the plastic to release
a pallid triangle of bread and egg
and chews on it a little and looks up,
and there are the trees doing nothing at all
but being oak and sycamore. She starts to notice
the corky heave of her lungs and bowel,
heart stomp, susurrus of blood,
and rises and balances back to the office
like an African woman, the whole sky on her head.

Parktime

As I went wanting
about the park, dawdling
after my need in the gritty walks,
squirrels were felting themselves
to the knuckles of trees

carrying their tails at a question
and not waiting but pitching
into verticals and riffs, till I saw
that it didn't matter a nut that this
was a deadletter day for answers,

so I ripped out all the photos
from the albums of thin air
and the pages of flimsy days
and trashed the lot, along with the my
and we and you and again you,

and my feet came free
to jink and shuffle in soft pine pins,
the hairs of my head to perk at leaves
and my ears at the brilliant lingo
of every common bird.

Theme and Variations

1.

Walls, white. Bath, white. Sky, white.
Tiles, black and white. Mat, black and white.
Cat, black almost, threaded
with white. My grandfather, upright,
threading the maze of white and black.

2.
A high white bentwood chair, seat patterned with holes.
Window, a frost of leaves.
My grandfather, parcelled in shirt and braces,
raises his chin christmassy with lather that he whisks
with a badgerhair brush.

The seaweed strip he keeps for telling the weather
will not release its frown,
but summer has bleached the shadows, and the cat
on the bath mat is waiting for his face to be washed
with his personal cloth.

3.
The cat's eye gleams
through a disc of light
like the white of an egg
glistening, slipped from the shell.
The rim of the bath
is solid eggwhite,
yolkless, grey inside.
My grandfather's head
is a hardboiled egg
in a cuff of speckled hair

My eyes behind my glasses
are doll's eyes, blue
on white. Dolly's eggs,
when the terracotta head
split open, tumbling
into the hard bath.

4.
My grandfather whistles rectangular songs.
Far down the invisible zigzag stairs,
someone is constructing pyramids of sound,
tall scales mantling and dismantling
with the opening and closing of a door,
diagonals, verticals, notes released
in chequers from a black and white box.
Blacksome Moses is measuring the day
with snow white kingly whiskers.

5.
Water is running. The sky is running blue.
My grandfather works delicately with knives,
reaping his chin or slicing a kingly roast
into translucent scallops. He can lay bare
the bones of tunes on a pinkish leather strop
or the sharpening steel, Baa Baa Black Sheep brisk
as a gypsy fiddler, honing the honed blade,
his cuffs pushed back. A vein in his wrist flexes
blue, and his eyes gleam up and his whiskers laugh.

6.
Sometimes it seems as though everything
is fixed, notated for ever. Chair
for lookout and waiting. The day spilled
or soured like milk. How a hand
may take hold of a wrist, up the stairs

down the stairs, the music measured out
in blacks and whites, and how we must dance
on the blade of a knife.
                        But the cat
is saying, Come on, I'll show you the door
to a garden where there's no black and white
but mine, and the only measure
is the span of my whiskers. Colours fall
like manna you never reserve, the sun
is a yolk for dipping and music a fountain,
and the weather grows green as it pleases.

Conversation Piece

Bolt upright on a comfortable chair
an aging patriot of sufficient means
passes the aromatic afternoons
in the address of a lady, coiffed, enhanced, mature.
"Madam, you know how greatly I admire
your passion, your acuity, your clear eye
unwavering like our friendship, your philosophy"
(etcetera. Slips to his usual theme, sour
and rebarbative.) "Jealousy alone,
not justice, overthrew me..."
                                    "Duty,
my dear sir. One does all that one can.
'Having done all, to stand.' A little tea?
The barbarian at the gate. This generation:
barbarity itself, do you not find?"
                        "You comfort me,

Madame! My memoirs shall record it:
you are the Cleopatra of your age!"
"Flattery, flattery! But time will judge.
That lesser men should denigrate
achievement: that's one's fate; one's lot!
Let history tell. Ignorant partisanship
and jealousy and spite will always carp –
but must not spoil, you know, our têtes à têtes."
        The afternoon has slipped into its dotage.
Saliva glistens on a mottled lip.
Beyond the window, foliage
nods in a vacant sky. She summons up
a wearying smile. "Courage,
mon cher ami. Come, let me fill your cup."

(Let us forgive one another
our past indiscretions
our inevitable corruptions
our present petites misères...
I do think Earl Grey is rather
insipid. People overrate –
Something on television
I had wished to record. The light –)
"Must it be au revoir? A little gin?
The evenings now... Yes, it is getting late.
Until we meet again.
Ah – your coat..."

Julie

There's the old woman at the window
half hidden behind the curtain waiting
for outofschool time stoking her fury
to leaking point and there are the kids
on the pavement sharp at a quarter to four
jeering and capering two fingers up
(weekends she's nothing to look forward to)

and there is Julie trailing behind
practising the angle of mumble (what
are you making faces for?) and thinking
of her Gran in the morning without teeth
and her distracted Mum the same wisps
and creases and the baby waving its fists
farting and mouthing with porridge on its chin.

The Ladies at Church

The ladies, two sad ladies,
The two sad floral ladies hung with stares,
Hung with beads and stares.

Their knuckles, heavy knuckles,
Their heavy washboard knuckles and their nails,
Ridged and bloodred nails.

The curtsey, prickled curtsey
Their Adam's apples made before the Lord,
Bobbing to the Lord

On Friday, helpless Friday
Before their naked Lord, the open-armed,
The mutilated, nailed, unseeing Lord.

Snow

Dorothy Wordsworth recorded the deaths in 1808 of George and Sarah Green
in a snowstorm as they were walking from Langdale to Grasmere.

The March night mouths out
a million syllables a million
deaf words hunting a syntax down
effaced crystals heaping
on every stone a fantasy of stone
over each invisible hill the perfect
husk of a hill imagined
and pins at an unfilled margin
the doodled shapes of man and woman
multiple strings of snow
plucking their legs crisscross slowdancing
a lost path home.

The fear that shocked their hearts awake
ticktack a Newton's Cradle
shrinks to a small hand rocking
writing and rocking penstrokes almost
upright a thumbstick in the drift
while snow raises the blanched
pile of a blanket over
her shawl his cloak and settles
sentence by sentence at their lips and eyes.

Visiting

Only fifty miles, but difficult. High ground,
low cloud, flooding at Appersett, roaming sheep.
Break at the mainroad factory shop
for coffee and a pee. Quick look round
for a splendid one-off tucked in the samples,
label discreetly slashed. Everything sick or bland.
Get to the ward. An hour to hold her hand
among suspended lives.
                          It's time – Oh yes
I know, because of the dog the driving
the dark the unfenced bits the cloud on hills.
Between the something and the something (I can't quote)
falls the shadow between dying and living
the shopping. About the angry pulse
that ticks at the throat of love, nobody writes a lot.

The Old Roads

Towards dusk or under light snow
the old roads reveal themselves
trodden into the hill
faltering at times in clay and gravel
gashed at a waterscour   picked up
as a strengthening scent   often their logic
cut by a counter logic
of intake walls   surefooted now
on a steady traverse   furrow
of descent   the cadence
abruptly lost

like the conversations
stitching our lives together
piecemeal so long   full
of inconsequences   laughs
digressions   forgetful pauses
abandonments   still in the old fashion
keeping in touch and always
working friendship deeper
that have come upon a stop
this jolt of severance
where no words find a footing

Any Fool Knows

Any fool knows,
she said, there's an increased risk.
The risk signing the air
with a slight blue flourish.

The way her throat
triumphed as the flame of a match
steadied to lend and the first
mycelia of smoke crept down,

tiniest upward
glory, sidewise slip of the look, discreet
public stab of bliss. The fruiting body
swelling, prepared to push.

Whether it was Love me
love my fag (they loved her), how she'd become
immune to certain words, or hellfire
preaching being out of fashion

along with repentance,
nobody said, For fuck's sake
you're costing me a packet. In any case
she won't be listening now.

A Change in the Weather

Worms that lay out in a soft dusk
are block-cold this morning. Frost
has burned them. Grass is grey,
sky a blank. Clothes I forgot
hang rigid on the line. I'm nonplussed
as if these are answers to questions
I had not known to ask; till my chilled hand
recalls her unresponsive cheek, the dead white
dress she would never have chosen.
It is the breaking of a dream. In I go
to write a letter I shan't send.

Taking Leave

When she was leaving
(taxi at the door, engine running)
he wrote, beyond speech,
(the familiar hand grown sketchy)
I didn't know you were going so soon.

And people leave, it's like that, always
sooner than they knew,
sooner that they thought, and things don't wait,
and a whole lifetime
isn't enough to discover the words.
Uncover, recover the words.

Speaking of the Dead

The moment when you say, Not any more.
Without pain or anger, something gives,
like a wrapping of ancient linen
or leather that is spent; and your eye
can gaze into a lost eye and feel
no rancour, because now it comprehends
how the first subtle binding was made.
Your freed hands stretch, unswaddled limbs,
and you laugh, learning the air and rain.

For a while these dead may search, fumbling
after lost authority. Dismiss them?
They fade of themselves, carrying no weight,
their language of command obsolescent.
You can feel for them, seeing how bruised,
powerless under their own dry constraints
and chafed they are; can love them, almost,
and leave them, busy at their mutual task
of burying and being buried.

On a Good Day for Hoeing

The young man came limping valentine pink
up the hill in his wellingtons. His hair
feathering in the wind like carrot leaves
was the rich orange of Danvers Half-Long
(old tapered variety, broadshouldered).

He sat down pot-bound in his cracked boots. Please
I could do with some veg. Cooked veg and bread.
Butter please if there is any butter,
not marg. When he pulled off the boots, his heels
were rubbed through the socks to the scarlet core.

He said Do you do WWOOFS at all? You know,
WWOOFS. Working Weekends On Organic Farms.
I could weed if you showed me. Look, those beds
could do with a weed. He laid himself down
in the fast-maturing vigorous sun.

You'll burn, I said. You're burnt already. Don't
go to sleep. But he was stretched damp and fast
in his compost jacket, beyond waking.
So I went in, and cut bread in the green
kitchen light, and pricked out the arguments,

and carried the whole cautious load outside
to his print in the flattened buttercups.
If he had stayed – But if no one shows you,
how do you tell a vagrant stripling god
from the groundsel, bittercress, burdock kind?

Persephone

At the corner of the eye. The corner of the lane.
Dark hair plastering her cheek. The skin of her arms
peaky cold. (April, and still no warmth
in the white sun.) Skimping shirt. She looks away,
chewing. It's like a film,
flashback to the mother (fleshy but still handsome)
abandoning everything for the search, distraught,
and such a winter. Five months, the girl turns up,
stows in her cheek whatever it is,
braces herself for kisses,
regular meals, the dressing of her hair. All summer
she looks sheepishly happy, her cheeks almost rosy.
She'll talk about clothes at times, express
preferences, but her eyes are tinged
with nettleroot yellow. You can tell
it won't last. She's bound to abscond. Submitting
once more to the gaze that knows her and mocks her,
to his greed and neglect, will be like downing
the first drink after an age
of abstinence. Nothing could be worse.
Nothing could be better.

Revenant

That pigjawed god with his thick phallus
who strolled into the garden, glimming
about with snailshell eyes,
crowdark among a sprawl of stems (how
could I swear that I saw him?) snatching
at nerine lilies and cardoon heads
and dragging boughs of half-ripe damsons down –
gone, when I turned my head.

But she, pleading some task, has risen
abruptly to go in. That shudder;
that red weal on her neck…
How the season is changing! we'll say,
drawing the curtains, loath to remark
on the plum trees, barked and scored, bleeding
new resin, or where something has plundered
the bees' nest in the wall .

Nanny Besom

There were witches when I was young.
Sometimes a light surprises   Door
cracks open   A solid figure
flits.   Is it you, Nanny Besom?

Taint of breath   Fingers pruned to pinch.
And let me see your tongue   Have we
been a good girl and have we been?
Whisking away my tears like crumbs.

Such scouring syrups. Nanny's eyes
are measuring spoons. Her barbed chin
trembles towards a north of guilt.
In winter, in the grey of it,

in the tallow sun, when sometimes
my heart's cold swells like ice in pipes
and I suffer the dull fraying
and uncoupling of life from hope,

she visits, a tarnished spirit.
In she slips, treading knuckled ground,
unwinding from her bag the death
I fear, unloving, clinical.

The Sick Woman Looks at her Eyes in the Mirror

Eyes dowsing through glass
for an assumed self can't reach it
outlong or in. Begin to drown
like fish immersed in ruinous air.

Some kind of defection? Mirror
looks hard back, assessing.
Chooses to reconstruct. Comes up
with pebbly striations,

voids half gritted in. Life here somewhere,
Self thinks, forcing forward. Beads!
Perforated bluish cylinders
you might buy in the souk,

or the fleamarket, corner of 75th,
poking through oddments, and the stallkeeper
rolling them in a seamed palm smiles
and says, These might be lucky.

Afternoon Off, 1936

We went to see the Film Star
Love is just around the corner
opening the Church Bazaar

With teeth of Japanese pearl
My heart stood still
a natural gloss on each neat fingernail

that Marcel wave
What is this thing called love?
and a waist you wouldn't believe

as though an angel were leaning out
Lovely to look at
from a silver frame with that celebrated pout

all purity of collar and piqué cuff
I need some cooling off
she bends towards us out of her life

in Hollywood California
I've got a crush on you (on her)
her voice tinier and tinnier

than you might suppose
Smoke gets in your eyes
and   Ladies an Gennelmen   declares

So delided this afternoon
How long has this been going on?
this er bizaar open

Lucky Dip Tombola
There's something in the air
Treasure Hunt Holeyboard Hoopla

Woodbine Black Cat candyfloss licorice
I never had a chance
lollipops rock cake coconut ice

and the Vicar flushed with worldly joy
It's de-lovely
with hands plump as a toad
wound the gramophone up to play
As time goes by
They can't take that away from me
in the sooty hall down Spring Grove Road

Alexandria: Days of 1895

The Irrigation Service (3rd Circle) of the Ministry of Public Works.
The Special Clerk, 29 years old, always reliable,
gathers the sheaves of paper, taps them together, files them,
pushes the key home, turns it. The collar is chafing his skin.
He is last to leave. Waft of sweet chestnut at the turn of the stairs.

He crosses the market and makes for the narrow streets he knows,
the reddish glow of doors half open, ochre of an upper window
silhouetting a turned shoulder, two inclined heads. Pulls out his watch
and, not to be late, hastens reluctantly to the evening's greetings,
fastidiously civil, the dull meal at his mother's table.

Pats at a pocket to feel the crackle of official paper
where his poem is drafted, makes his excuses and escapes
to the single candle of his room to refine what he has written
and note down the dream of what he observed
on the stained street.

Dinka Labourers in Khartoum

At dusk they entered the garden
wrapped in their indigo rags, stalking
as delicately as crowned cranes
to join their men,

and crouched under the wall, long limbs
like the folded wings of bats, the glint
of silver at a wrist, the gleam
of downcast smiles,

and lowered slings from their shoulders
to the cool dust. Peeled away cloths. Pot,
sticks, bread, pouch of millet, sleeping
face of a child.

Their words were single twigs, fed in
to the little fire. The men lay still,
picks put by, heads on folded arms;
and then one sang,

perhaps of the price of a bride,
a beaded forehead, flight of a spear,
savour of flesh above embers,
a humped white bull.

There was the pale gecko pausing
and pausing on the shadowy wall,
and there was the lamp, and the dust
under the lamp,

and the smell of bitter orange
seeping from the dark, and the music
of exile north or south, and loss,
and lack of kin.

The Locusts

Once on a morning without sky
I opened the shutters to a clay sun.
My naked footprints marked a trail from cot
to window in the dust. Dust blurred the walls,
trees, roofs, the whole deadened city
as I peered into the fatigue of the day.

Out of the desert, locusts ranged
in a husky tissue of wings, and folded
among citrus trees, clipped upright to each stem,
their hungers rustling like hail.
Each gazed at nothing out of a polished eye;
and lifted abruptly over the spoils
of ruined leaves, spindling, spindling away
like the breaking of a fever.

Sometimes my buried memories pupate,
hatch in my throat, cling with a hooked foot,
gather me into their malachite stare,
show me a child, his breath harsh and gauzy,
eyelids the colour of a bruise
and an alabaster body, burning.

Model and Photographer

Grand Central Station, New York City 1999

Has left herself off
somewhere along with
makeup money keys,
a T shirt maybe,
stepped into the skin
of a nymph (tissue
of palest suede, holes
for the eyes), gleaming
taffeta, matt silk,
scallops of veined stone
spread under her feet.
Ready? Go now Go
and he reels her taut
against a swept kelp
of bodies moving
Go girl don't mind them
hauling her silvers
over the concourse
over and over
till the line frays out
the fans of marble
dissolve and she trips,
her startled face still
almost deserted.

Hurricane Edge

New York 1999

A leaf bobbed like a float.
First stipple on dusty slabs. Peck
on the cheek, the childish kiss
of rain. Kiss the shining rods of rain.
The lish beat filled. A canvas sky,
slung between buildings, darkened, sagged,
came suddenly unsheeted.

Some ran. Some, what could we do
but stand in the downdrag, thinned,
punched through like zinc?
Hair smeared to the scalp
like trodden grass, we gazed
at the eelback thresh of gutters,
tranced to the bone with rain.

A yellow pickup
hacked into water, shoaled it
rim over rim in blowsy fans,
rode through on throbbing din, got out –
just – on the swash, left us
blasted, heads wide open
like dynamited fish,

shocked into knowing that rain
could build to a bulging cornice
and it would happen: scribbled cracks
in plaster mouthing open, trees
and houses gaping and losing grip,
rampage of sullen water,
cries under the wind.

And now the city's dazed,
still gingerly balanced, footfast
in pulpy ground, up to its pulse
in trash; but we can walk
on a willowpattern sky, threading
the squares and streets together,
putting the horizons back.

We've found our rhythm, dryshod
passacaglia, ordinary present.
We could go shopping. Only
we've seen the news, the paper's here
with photos of cockeyed roofs, woods
broomed down, sprawling cars, a logjam
in North Carolina of drowned sows.

We've read some names. Yet we're baptised,
for reasons we can't fathom,
into belief in safety, sitting
at the right hand of luck, able
for now to tell our nearly tales,
reprieved; while a fist in a pocket
stays closed on a sprig of guilt.

Sightseers in New York City (1999)

A technological marvel
to stand in an earthconditioned box
and be rocketed multiple ceilings

above grave level. There should be
revelations, lightness. You'd expect
the body not to recognize itself;

and yet the stolid heart goes on
beating the same drum. Somebody's guts
mumbled; the air was charged with aftershave.

Less dramatic than witnessing
the money capsule ping round the wires
in Palmer's shop to the goddess cashier

(and that was in nineteen forty)
only this time we are the small change
dropped in, and it's a vertical hurtle,

sans gods because we're democrats
and everybody has the same right
to the same miniaturised amazements:

the toy cars going and stopping,
the random moves of dots we assume
to resemble ourselves, the crumpled sea

printed with the white V's of wakes
pinned to invisible ships, the flat
diorama of a world diminished.

But close by stood the young black man
in his loose business suit and good shoes,
gesturing like a dancer, pointing out

to his visiting folks just where
he lived above the deli, his route
to work, and where they had left their new bags,

meeting their proud astonished eyes,
patting their shoulders, reassuring,
knowing his place, at home and still as large

as life. And they gazed down over
the broad avenues of Manhattan,
smiling at casual pigeons swimming lengths.

Like a Mote in the Eye

New York City 2001

Like a mote in the eye,
Like someone far off, waving,
red top white trousers, a tiny woman
diagram of a woman figure X.

Like somebody you knew
(or was it a film), smiling,
crossing the office floor with documents
ambitions newly washed hair, and meanwhile

the plane on a straight course,
carapace of the building
unresistant like flesh under the axe.
The skin divides revealing the shocked meat.

Somebody's camera
(it's a reflex, you just shoot)
recording this neat forked doll-dancer poised
against the air how many storeys up,

tiny and very clear,
very clearly defined, there,
a scrap in a hollow tooth that a tongue
is about to seize on and flip away.

Child and Toad

She would lean and reach in
to the hollow root slowly
as far as her elbow
and stroke the toad's chin

and in the waiting afternoon
he would carry his yellow bulk
out of his place of dark
to throb in the unwanted sun

giving his eyes to light,
his cool pale pads of toes
his mouth lipless and wordless
and the skin of his throat.

If the ancient stump
is there lodged in the bank
of the leafy paddock
where we made our camp,

perhaps he still crouches
breathing secret hours,
days, seasons, years,
still dozes, still watches

the light's transformation
from his earthy seat
beside the hollow lane.
Hunker down, toad.
She won't come again.
Hunker down, heart.

Taking It In

About cuckoo-time in the bit of copse
she warned my shadow. Clap of my heart
startled both our skins. While I stood prickling
she mapped me with her tongue.

The babble and challenge of the morning
fell to a breath. I became a tree
and the sun had time to spread on the bank
while she assessed my heat.

As we grew softer to one another
she showed me her belly distended
with children, narrow godlets, and drew them
over the oakleaf crumb

without haste towards some brackeny dark
and vanished. Birdsong streamed back. The light
she had worn like a membrane found its place
on leaves and beads of grit.

She left no trace but in my head. Tell me,
Maker of serpents, how many lives
I shall need to swallow the whole world's egg
without spilling a drop.

Snail

Snail pearls footlucid from the infant cluster,
eases to a vegetable deep, mouthing
his trawl, his greenlit mumble.

Unfurls a muscle of his foraging eye
and coasts like a swan in shadow,
mushing his meat of leaves.

Once, painted my spread palm with his
on an upward slicksilver piste, and showed me
how the world hangs and pulses;

and will disc himself in, cellar his kiss
all winter, build his occlusions
like the bowl of a fine horn spoon.

The Fox in the Borren

I had stayed late at the embers
of the heavy sun. Suddenly
he was there, dog fox haunched on a boulder,
come to survey his night.

He knew how to be still, forepaws
set in the stance of a pharaoh,
muzzle and ears high, savouring the broad
incoming tide of dark.

I watched. He waited. Then I saw
discomfiture creep to his neck
and arch it, and flow the length of his spine.
He knew himself observed.

The last rays twitched in pelt and brush.
He stood, and was away quick march
from the sense of me, stone by stone, angry.
I had stripped him of ease

and driven him into some porch
of the tumbled borren, as dusk
drove me, half frightened, to make for the rank
tunnel of human light.

I imagine his play,
his quick, casual mating;
and recall one distant midnight
in the city, lying awake,
when that first time I heard a vixen scream,
scouring the concrete pastures, hot for life.

Signs

The sky's all wrung silk and smooth bellies
of cloud. There's a sense of waiting. I know
what that means, we're in for rain. Paul
stops at the gate, brown face in a grin,
and pushes his cap, white forehead (it's like
peeling a nice boiled egg), crosses
his big yellow boots, that means we're in
for talk. Behind him down at the field edge
there's magpies cavorting, I can't
just tell how many, six or seven,
how does the rhyme go? Paul's saying next time
it'll be Labour for certain
and we're in for a hard winter, look
at the hawthorn, you can tell, and his wife,
not sure yet but they think it's twins.

Field Head

Strolling to Field Head in the afternoon
I stepped into fog like the kind of ghost
that walks through walls. A dimension had slipped
from the world. There was only density,
less or more, and slowness, a monochrome
clinging. A cow that raised her head to stare
was snipped out of gauze. The field was moonlit
without any moon. We were all shadows,
our substance leached away, and the ground flowed
beneath us, post, tree, grass, woman, cow, stone.

Down at the gate an old dog was waving
his shadow tail and barking a raspy
rundown bark. Invisible water spoke
in an urgent whisper. Oh I needed
to be solid again, and waded back
to the breathing upper air. A tractor
was working near Argill House. A wren bobbed
on the wall. There sat the foxcoloured sun,
and the green grass was bloomed with a thousand
thousand silver spidery empty nets.

Selling Up

The last are gone. I have called up
the yellow heifers from the field
with their coats crisp against winter
and sold them away. It is gain and loss.
Their absence is like a fasting.

This morning a rainbow planted
its shaft full into the cropped grass
and I thought foolishly of Noah
alone in the ark, an empty bucket
in his hand and nothing to do,

and wondered what he would have missed
the most, hay smells or slop and steam
of dung, or the way the old cow
could speak under her breath to the new calf,
or a curled yellow poll to scratch.

Gift Horse

Old roan Rose. Tom Harvey
begged her, wall-eyed mare
with a rope and a feedbag saddle,
bound for the knacker's. The hired lad
pocketed a ten bob note, grinned,
rubbed his bum and was gone.

Hauled left and left, the bit dragged
half out of her mouth, she'd miss
the granite stoop by a grassblade,
knuckling uphill, feet stamping,
tail pinned stiff, her milky eye
cocked madly towards home;

and home veered always
away like the sidling elusive
foot of a rainbow. She'd work,
jouncing scrawny quarters, neck
pumphandling, throwing her breast
to the collar in her heart's reprieve.

She's long ago fed hounds, and Tom's
bulk been eased to ground. Where
the shoddy barn stood, a road
swerves in a double arc, skirting
the galled and speckled moor, intent
on pitching somewhere better.

On the Way Down

An old ewe kesent among rushes, lodged
belly up in her blanket of dirty fleece,
cleft stare fixed on dying.

Our fists clenching deep into ragged wool
couldn't haul her up to rights. Only her fear
buckled her back to life

and sent her lurching from the smell of us
and the alien voices, out of our hands,
till at last she settled

to the sweet rummage of grass. Months, perhaps;
maybe a spring to nourish a spindling lamb.
So we took on the fleece

of doubtful weather, looking back at times,
and followed the harsh track down. One more season?
We are making old bones.

Going West

A long distance from anywhere
you might remember. The last trees
were a while back. The hedges
sit tight, leaning inland. The air starts
to stick to your tongue and the map
reaches a final name.

There isn't very much to do, although
if you don't park with your back to the sea
you can glimpse Scotland when the cloud lifts,
so someone's troubled to work
on the notice until it advises

Please d i e carefully. Jack's Surf Bar
is where they discuss the perfect
wave. There was a perfect wave
once, and at Jack's
it goes on rolling, Pacific blue,
crested and glassy, chariot of heroes.

Bingo was last Thursday. There is the Ship
and the Grapes. Before long, the surly sea
that is fed dropped chips and ice cream
will prowl and starve, the Leisure Centre have
more leisure that it can afford

and if you crunch out over the shingle
you can tell that the earth is flat.
Away down the coast, white masts
are fulling the salty air.
A solitary cormorant
tautens his line of flight

unerring over the keen waterchop,
fastening southerly to northerly,
one hard cusp of distance to another.
Two dogs with experienced grey muzzles
are laughing over something.

This is a place for men
and miniature men, for talk
of tides catches records goals. The women
sit. Older sitters have good big teeth,
and heads grown white like the blackheaded gulls
resigned to August.

(You don't expect a lad like the one down there,
the blue puffajacket, to be sitting alone,
his head bowed so low you might wonder,
but no it's all right, clamped
to his ear there's a mobile phone.)

This is a place to practise
the fine skills of waiting,
for a call, an encounter, a tug
on the line, for better luck; where almost
any pebble could turn out,
given an eye to discern it,

a wrist to flick it one step further
than the edge of the known the ledged
brown world, to be a champion skipper,
could abandon once and for all the kingdom
of tearooms and a ragwort sun.

Late Snow

An end. Or a beginning.
Snow had fallen again and covered
the old dredge and blackened mush
with a gleaming pelt; but high up there
in the sycamore top, Thaw
Thaw, the rooks cried,
sentinel by ruined nests.

Water was slacking into runnels
from drifts and pitted snowbacks,
dripping from the gutter and ragged
icicle fringes. Snow paused
in the shining embrace of bushes,
waiting in ledged curds and bluffs
to tumble into soft explosions.

And suddenly your absence
drove home its imperatives like frost,
and I ran to the high field
clumsily as a pregnant woman
to tread our names in blemished
brilliant drifts; because the time we have
is shrinking away like snow.

Letters 1

I lived here once. Oh, and I am still
unlocking the door, wiping my boots,
switching the light on, hanging my coat
on the newel post, greeting the cat.
Yes, and picking up the mail. People
still write, and I answer. But someone
has moved. Somebody I thought I was,
who fitted my clothes, left last summer
without any forwarding address.

Letters 2

You say how strange it seems that I never
write about you, my sons and my daughters.
I hear your unspoken reproach: Don't we
matter as much as...? And I can't explain.
I can't say, when I heard you at the door,
how eagerly I ran to light the fire
and set places for you and cut the bread.
I had reached that house only days before.
You arrived, pilgrims, wanderers, swallows,
magi witnessing your own holy birth,
a flock of the wild migrant geese, gypsies.
You took food. The time came when we went on,
each alone. We had grasped a few phrases
of each others' language, hardy enough
for greetings and goodbyes. Go well now! Look
at the immense distances we travel,
rushing away from each other like stars.

You Words

Inherited, not mine,
mine to mistrust and learn,

you are indifferent to me.
I wake as you pace by.

You are key to this locked room.
I am queen to your swarm.

Child at the breast,
Clue that will wind to a beast,

Kiss to my long sleep,
necessary rape,

rain to my drought,
my bletted timber breeds your sudden fruit.

Your clear curd forms in my thin whey.
I am the berry, you the supping fly.

You are guardian to my peace,
fox to my henhouse.

You words that quest, voice, check, run
like hounds hunting alone,

blade to my dirty wound,
I am the means to your end.

The Twelve Pavilions

To, fro, the drummers go,
Midnight, midday,
Drumming the year away.
Eleven pipers piping hot,
A frieze of lords to pay the scot.
One lord skips as
Drunk as a lord may be
Without any lady.

Nine musing ladies dance like stars,
Like planets in long ellipses.
Along the invisible Milky Way
They danced all day.
Eight little maids with buckets and spades,
Seven enchanted boys.
Six geese squabbling made such noise
The Queen of the Realm could bear it no longer.
Out she ran with a ring on each finger
Of her golden hand,
Swept them out of the land.

Caqueux Caqueux they flew
To Gascony and Poitou,
Collibert Collibert calling with every breath.
My dears! I am frightened to death!
Said the little French Hens and nodded their spangled heads.
There will be storms! There will be wars!
Nodding and babbling.
Two turtle doves sang soft and high,
You be Cantoris, I'll be Decani.
My heart is broken, coo, coo.
How sad! How true!

And all this time a partridge sat
In the pear tree wobbling
On unaccustomed toes.
This is the way the music goes.
My true love searched in winter heat
And summer snows
Through all the twelve pavilions of the year,
But I wasn't there.